ASSYRIAN EMPIRE

A History from Beginning to End

Copyright © 2019 by Hourly History.

Table of Contents

Introduction

The Assyrian Empire came to dominate the ancient Near East as it grew into the most powerful of all the Mesopotamian empires. At its height, it covered all of Mesopotamia and reached as far north as Asia Minor (modern-day Turkey) and as far south as Egypt. It used a sophisticated centralized bureaucracy to control its captured lands and people, new military strategies and tactics to defeat its foes, and brutal and violent repression to deter anyone who considered standing against it.

From around 2000 BCE to 600 BCE, this empire was one of the most important drivers of political, military, and social change in the civilized world. The story of the Assyrian Empire can be divided into three parts, each of which involved a rise and subsequent fall and each of which was more powerful and more far-reaching than what had come before. These three stages of the Assyrian Empire are known to historians as the Old Empire, the Middle Empire, and the Late Empire (also known as the Neo-Assyrian Empire). Each has its own story, its own cast of characters, and its own timeline of triumph and defeat. Taken together, these provide an account of one of the longest-lasting empires the world has ever seen.

Amongst many other achievements, the Assyrian Empire introduced the Aramaic alphabet. This was easier to write than the Akkadian language which preceded it, and it became the standard language not just of the empire but most of the civilized world. Some historians claim that the introduction of this new alphabet is the single most important and lasting legacy of the Assyrian Empire since it is the forerunner of the modern Arabic and Hebrew alphabets. It also means that, through study of documents written in this language, we know a great deal about the Assyrian Empire.

Chapter One

Origins

"The hammer shatters glass but forges steel."

—Mesopotamian proverb

Mesopotamia, the fertile area between the Tigris and Euphrates Rivers, has been described as the cradle of civilization. Here for the first time, humans developed from nomadic hunter-gatherers into sophisticated city builders. Here for the first time, there was planned agriculture and irrigation, the keeping of livestock, and the development of bronze tools and weapons. Here too was the first development of wheeled vehicles and canals. Without the changes which took place in this area beginning around 3000 BCE, the modern world in which we live simply wouldn't exist.

First came the Sumerians, outsiders who arrived in this area at around the beginning of the third millennium BCE. No one knows where they came from, but they were very different from the nomadic tribes who had previously populated these lands. The Sumerians (this name comes from *sang-ngiga*, meaning "the black heads," the name they used to describe themselves) were ethnically different from the local people and spoke a different language. They also brought with them some very different ideas. First of all, these were farmers who appreciated the value of the fertile land and the importance of creating irrigation channels to distribute water from the rivers. Previously, the people who lived here moved from place to place, following game and the seasonal appearance of fruit and berries. The Sumerian farmers were very different—they didn't need to move around because they grew their food close to their homes. This meant that they weren't forced to live in portable wood and skin tents—they could build permanent homes made initially from bundles of reeds smeared with river mud but later from more durable mud bricks.

With ample food being produced by their farms, the Sumerian villages grew into cities, and a whole new class of people appeared for the first time: artisans, who did not need to spend their time producing food but could instead specialize in things like metalwork and construction. They might not have looked as complex and sophisticated as modern cities, but these were the very first urban centers created by humans. Before long, the whole of southern Mesopotamia was covered in a network of Sumerian city-states, each with its own ruler, religion, and society. All these city-states used the Sumerian language in written and spoken form and, despite frequent clashes between cities, no one city came to completely dominate the others.

The Sumerians also developed trade with other parts of the Near East. Although Mesopotamia was a good place to grow food, it was short of other resources such as timber and metal ores. These were traded with societies as far away as the Indus River Valley in India.

By 2500 BCE, there were around half a million Sumerians, and about 80% of these people lived in their mighty cities which at this time included Uruk, Kish, Nippur, Lagash, Umma, and Ur. The two most powerful of these cities were Umma and Lagash, and there were a number of fights between the two for control of southern Mesopotamia. However, around 2300 BCE, a young man who had been a cupbearer to the king of Umma became the leader of a new group of Semitic-speaking people from the north of Mesopotamia who took control of all of the Sumerian cities. This young man, who gave himself the title King Sargon ("the legitimate king"), set about building an empire that eclipsed everything the Sumerians had achieved.

Under the rule of Sargon (who quickly became known as Sargon the Great), what became known as the Akkadian Empire grew in power and influence. The Akkadian language replaced Sumerian both in the Sumerian cities and in the other lands conquered by Sargon. For 150 years, the Akkadian Empire, ruled by Sargon and his descendants, was the most powerful on the planet. It ruled lands into Iran, Syria, and as far as Egypt and the shores of the Mediterranean Sea. Within the Akkadian Empire, there was a great explosion of art, including some of the first literature and poetry and a growing interest in science (especially astronomy) and medicine. This empire also saw the development of standardized weights and measures, a single system of laws for all its citizens, improvements in infrastructure including roads and canals, the introduction of the very first postal system, and the building of a trade empire that stretched across the Near East and Asia.

Just when it appeared to be so powerful that no one could stand against it, the Akkadian Empire collapsed, partially due to a long-lasting drought and subsequent famines which swept through Mesopotamia and beyond. When Shu-turul, the last king of Akkad, was deposed in 2154 BCE, the area descended into anarchy as the Gutians, a warlike hill tribe from the Zagros Mountains, swept across Mesopotamia. Many Sumerian cities regained their independence by paying tribute to the Gutians. The Akkadian people who had formed the ruling class of the Akkadian Empire went both to the south and north. In the south, they went to the city of Babylon, which would itself become the center of an empire. In the north, they congregated in the city of Ashur on the west bank of the Tigris River in the north of modern-day Iraq.

The nomadic Gutians proved to have no interest in farming or even in occupying the land they dominated. In time, they retreated back to their mountain strongholds in the Zagros Mountains. With the fragmentation of the Akkadian Empire, it was only a matter of time before another empire filled the power vacuum in Mesopotamia.

Chapter Two

The City of Ashur

"The Assyrian came down like the wolf on the fold,
And his cohorts were gleaming in purple and gold."

—Lord Byron

The city of Ashur (also known as Aššur) was located on a plateau above the Tigris River in what is now al-Shirqat District in northern Iraq. This location had been inhabited from the earliest times—some archeologists have discovered remains which suggest that there was a city of permanent houses there as early as 3000 BCE. However, it doesn't seem to have been until the beginning of the second millennium BCE that this became a major city-state. The city shared its name with the main deity worshipped there—the god Ashur, who was represented by a winged disc or sun. Like most city-states of this period, the city had its own ruler but his jurisdiction did not extend far beyond the city walls.

The earliest people who ruled the city were referred to in contemporary and later texts as "the kings who lived in tents," which suggests a lifestyle in the early years of the city that was as least partly nomadic. During its early years, the city was dominated by the Sumerian cities to the south. Several accounts of the activities of Sumerian kings, especially Eannatum of Lagash, the dominant Sumerian king in the 26th century BCE, mention conflict with *Subartu* (the Sumerian name for the lands which would become Assyria), and several cities in Subartu are noted as paying tribute to the Sumerians.

When Sumer was taken over by Sargon the Great and his Akkadian followers, Ashur also became part of the Akkadian Empire. Under the rule of Sargon, the city was enlarged, new temples were built, and many traders and merchants came to the city. When the Akkadian Empire collapsed, Ashur regained some form of independence, and it seems to have avoided the worst effects of the drought and famine which affected large parts of Mesopotamia; in the period 2200 to 2000 BCE, several large cities in the area were completely abandoned, seemingly as a direct consequence of the drought. Around 2100 BCE, Ashur became part of the Third Dynasty of Ur (also known as the Neo-Sumerian Empire).

The city-state of Ashur seems to have been mainly a trading center. It lay on one of the most important trade routes in the ancient world which stretched from Anatolia to Mesopotamia and on to the Levant. Thousands of clay cuneiform tablets have been recovered and deciphered, and these tell us a great deal about the situation in the early part of the city's history. These records tell us that the plains around the city were used to raise large flocks of sheep. The wool from these animals then became one of the main resources traded by the city.

Wealthy merchants from Ashur set up a trading post in the ancient Anatolian city of Kanesh (or Kaneš). There were many such trading posts during that period, but Kanesh became one of the most important in the early growth of the city of Ashur. The city of Kanesh was ruled by the Hattians, and part of the city was given over to the karum, a secure area where merchants from Ashur could bring their goods in exchange for paying taxes to the king of the city (the word *karum* means "port" in Akkadian). Merchants from Ashur brought wool and clothing to Kanesh and exchanged these for silver, tin, spices, and luxury items. The merchants in Kanesh were protected by soldiers from Ashur, who were permitted as long as they stayed within the confines of the karum.

Many families from Ashur established outposts in Kanesh, leaving behind trusted family members who supervised trade with the locals and the dispatch of goods back to Ashur. This had the effect of bringing great wealth into Ashur. One scholar of the ancient world has noted that "for several generations the trading houses of Karum Kanesh flourished, and some became extremely wealthy— ancient millionaires."

The wealth flowing into Ashur from trade not only brought luxury to a few; it was also used to improve and expand the city itself. Although its position on a high, steep-sided plateau made Ashur relatively easy to defend, high walls were built around it to make it even safer. The city became a vital link in the expanding trade between Mesopotamia and Anatolia. The import of tin from Anatolia also gave metalworkers in the city the opportunity to perfect their working of iron, and iron tools and weapons created in Ashur soon became famous for their quality and strength.

It wouldn't be long before the city of Ashur would need these superior weapons to protect its position as a trading hub of the ancient world.

Chapter Three

The Old Kingdom

"If you go and take the field of an enemy, the enemy will come and take your field."

—Mesopotamian proverb

By 2050 BCE, the Third Dynasty of Ur was beginning to fragment and the city-state of Ashur was finally able to achieve full independence. At this time, the rulers of Ashur did not refer to themselves as kings; their usual title was governor (*ensi* in Sumerian). The first known ruler of the independent city of Ashur was said to have been Ushpia, who was one of the first Assyrian rulers to make the transition from a semi-nomadic to a fully urbanized life. Ushpia is also credited as the first ruler to build a temple to the god Ashur in the city. We know the names of the four subsequent rulers of Ashur: Apiashal, Sulili, Kikkia, and Akiya, but we almost nothing else about their lives or reigns other than that the city walls were enlarged and strengthened sometime before 2025 BCE.

At that time a new ruler took over in the city of Ashur, Puzur-Ashur I (the name means "servant of Ashur"). Like the preceding rulers, Puzur-Ashur I styled himself governor rather than king, and it appears that, unlike most of the other city-states in Mesopotamia which were ruled by autocratic and powerful kings, the ruler of Ashur was supported by some form of council which assisted with the setting of laws and policies. Puzur-Ashur I founded a dynasty that would rule the city for eight generations and passed on the rule of Ashur to his son, Shalim-ahum.

Under the Puzur-Ashur dynasty, the city-state of Ashur continued to thrive and trade with Anatolia remained the main source of wealth. However, even without the Akkadian or Neo-Sumerian Empires, there were a number of threats facing the city. These included the Hittites, the Hurrians, the Mitanni, and the Elamites. The Hittites and the Hurrians were confederations of tribes from north-central Anatolia. The kingdom of Mitanni was located in an area in northern Syria and southeast Anatolia. Elam was an ancient kingdom centered in what is now the far west and southwest of Iraq, and the Elamites took advantage of the fall of the Third Dynasty of Ur to try to expand their sphere of influence. At various times, all these entities tried to encroach on Assyrian trading routes and centers in Anatolia. All caused problems, but all were successfully repulsed. However, there was another group that was far more of a menace to the city-state of Ashur: the Amorites.

The Amorites are mentioned in Sumerian texts as early as 2400 BCE, but in around 2200 BCE, they began a mass migration into lands which were first part of the Akkadian Empire and then ruled by the Third Dynasty of Ur. It seems possible that the same drought which had caused a catastrophic decline in the Akkadian Empire may also have prompted the Amorites to leave their traditional homelands in what is now Jebel Bishri in northern Syria to seek more fertile lands in which to graze their herds.

The Amorites infiltrated a number of Mesopotamian city-states. They did this in general not by fighting, but by settling in the host cities until they were strong enough to supplant the ruling classes with Amorites. In many cases, wealthy Amorite grain merchants gradually increased their power within a particular city until they were strong enough to support their own nomination for the throne. In this way, many Sumerian and former Akkadian city-states became ruled by Amorites. By the nineteenth century BCE, influential cities including Larsa, Lagash, and Babylon were ruled by Amorite groups. Before long, the Amorites were also looking at the wealthy northern city of Ashur.

At this time, Ashur was ruled by Erishum II, a direct descendant of Puzur-Ashur I. By now, the rulers of Ashur had started to use the title king, but Erishum II would be the last king of the Puzur-Ashur dynasty. In 1809 BCE, Erishum II was deposed and replaced by a new king of Ashur, Shamshi-Adad I. We know nothing about the circumstances in which the new king took the throne, but we do know that Shamshi-Adad I was an Amorite and that he immediately began strengthening his city.

The city walls were once again enlarged and made stronger, the first Great Royal Palace was built for the new king, and the temple of Ashur was extended and improved, including the addition of a large ziggurat (stepped pyramid). Outside the city, the new king united other cities in the area under the control of Ashur. These included Arbel, Nineveh, and Arrapkha, and this gave Ashur control of a small area between the Tigris and Euphrates Rivers, including a part of the Zagros Mountains. With these core cities secure, Shamshi-Adad I was able to more easily protect the Assyrian trade routes against incursions.

Satisfied with his achievements, Shamshi-Adad I awarded himself the rather optimistic title "King of the Universe" and built a new capital city on the site of an existing small town, Shekhna in the Khabur River basin in what is now northeastern Syria. The new city was called Shubat-Enlil ("home of the god Enlil" in Akkadian), and it included a palace complex, a temple to Enlil, and a planned residential area. The whole city was surrounded by a large wall but lacked the natural defenses of Ashur which was located on a steep-sided plateau.

The next target for Shamshi-Adad I was the city of Mari, an important trade center that controlled the main caravan route between Mesopotamia and Anatolia. In 1795 BCE, King Yahdun-Lim of Mari was assassinated, possibly by his own servants (and perhaps with the encouragement of Shamshi-Adad I) and his heir fled. Shamshi-Adad I occupied the city and installed one of his sons, Yasmah-Adad, as king of Mari. Then, Shamshi-Adad I turned his attention to the large city of Ekallatum, on the left bank of the Tigris River, south of Ashur. This was also conquered, and Shamshi-Adad's other son, Ishme-Dagan, was installed as king.

Shamshi-Adad I then allied himself with King Dadusha of the Sumerian city-state of Eshnunna, and the two attacked and conquered the area between the Zab rivers. With the campaign successfully completed, Shamshi-Adad I then turned on his former ally and conquered the cities of Shaduppum and Nerebtum. By 1780 BCE, King Shamshi-Adad I had carved out a large empire which encompassed

Upper Mesopotamia, Anatolia, and much of modern-day Syria. Shamshi-Adad I awarded himself the title "King of All," a title formerly used by the great Akkadian leader Sargon the Great. This empire was known as the Kingdom of Upper Mesopotamia, and only later was it referred to as the Old Kingdom or Old Assyrian Empire.

Shamshi-Adad I certainly seems to have been a ferociously able leader. In military matters, he was extremely knowledgeable (especially about siege warfare), and all his military actions were very carefully planned. Under his rule, incursions into his territory were finally ended completely. He was also a meticulous organizer of everything in his kingdom from matters of high state policy down to the provision of supplies for his troops. He also employed a network of spies who reported back directly to him and used what we would now call propaganda to make sure everyone heard about his successes. Shamshi-Adad I allowed many of the cities and areas he conquered to retain their own unique religious practices, and in some cities (Nineveh, for example) large temples were built using state funding.

Under this capable ruler, the Old Assyrian Empire thrived. Trade with Anatolia continued and new conquests meant that more profit flowed into the empire. The king's sons, however, were evidently less focused than their father. There were many messages from the king to his sons, often complaining about their behavior. One, to his son Yasmah-Adad, the ruler of Mari, indignantly notes, "While here your brother is victorious, down there you lie about among the women." Another letter scolds, "Are you a child, not a man, have you no beard on your chin?"

When Shamshi-Adad I died in 1776 BCE and was replaced by his son, Ishme-Dagan I, many of his enemies took the opportunity to turn against the empire. The king of Eshnunna launched an attack that took back much of the land taken by Shamshi-Adad I and even captured cities close to Ashur. The new king's brother, Yasmah-Adad, was ejected from Mari and the Semitic kingdom of Yamkhad from what is now Aleppo in Syria attacked several provinces of the kingdom. Yet the greatest threat to the Old Assyrian Empire came from the south, from the Amorite-controlled city-state of Babylon, which was growing in power.

Ishme-Dagan I had faced a growing threat from Babylon, especially after a new, young and ambitious king, Hammurabi, took the throne there in 1792 BCE. By 1755 BCE, the Babylonians under Hammurabi had conquered most of Mesopotamia and had defeated the armies of the Old Assyrian Empire in a number of large battles. The city of Shubat-Enlil was besieged and destroyed, and the capital of what remained of the empire once more reverted to Ashur.

By the time that Ishme-Dagan's son and successor, Mut-Ashkur, took the throne in 1730 BCE, he inherited little more than the city of Ashur and a few vassal city-states in the immediate vicinity including Nineveh. The empire carved out by Shamshi-Adad I had vanished, but the core cities remained safe and secure.

Chapter Four

The Middle Assyrian Empire

"The strong live by their own wages; the weak by the wages of their children."

—Mesopotamian proverb

For more than 300 years, the city-state of Ashur remained a small but wealthy trading center. When the Babylonian Empire fell to the Hittites around 1600 BCE, Ashur was able to retain its independence. The rise of the newly founded Mitanni Empire in the mid-1500s BCE to the northwest also seems to have had little effect on the city beyond a requirement to pay tribute. Even the resurgence of Kassite Babylon to the south does not seem to have threatened what remained of the empire. A series of astute kings used alliances and intermarriage to ensure their independence without conflict, and the cities of Ashur and Nineveh became wealthy and secure.

Then, in around 1392 BCE, the Mitanni Empire, which had become the most powerful in the region, became entangled in a dispute over the succession. The king of Ashur, Eriba-Adad I, took advantage of this instability to install a pro-Assyrian faction in the Mitanni court, increasing Assyrian influence over the Mitanni Empire.

When he was succeeded by his son Ashur-uballit I in 1365 BCE, the new king of Ashur would feel confident enough to take on the Mitanni Empire and to build the foundations of what would become one of the most powerful empires the world had ever seen.

Ashur-uballit I began by attacking the forces of the Mitanni Empire under the command of their new king, Shuttarna II. In a large-scale battle, the Assyrian forces were triumphant which allowed Ashur-uballit I to occupy lands previously held by the Mitanni, though he stopped short of attempting a full-scale invasion of the Mitanni homelands. In a short time, the Assyrian king also inflicted major military defeats on the Hittites, leaving Assyria dominant in northern Mesopotamia and Kassite Babylon as the only other major power in the area.

The Babylonians sought to avoid conflict with the growing new empire and instead formed an alliance with the Assyrians. To re-enforce this alliance, the Kassite king of Babylon married the daughter of Ashur-uballit I. This link between the ruling houses of both empires ensured peace in the short-term, but it angered many people in Babylon. They were concerned about what they considered as an undue and growing Assyrian influence on Babylon, and a small cabal of plotters reacted by murdering the Babylonian king and replacing him with their own man.

Infuriated by the rebellion, Ashur-uballit I took his army into southern Mesopotamia and attacked Babylon. The Babylonian forces were quickly and completely defeated, and the plotters were executed. Ashur-uballit I then installed a new king, Kurigalzu II, on the throne in Babylon. The city of Babylon was not occupied and, at least nominally, it remained independent. However, by showing that he was able to replace the king at will, Ashur-uballit I ensured that Babylon remained under Assyrian control.

Ashur-uballit I then turned his attention back to the Mitanni Empire which had been severely weakened by battles over the succession following the death of King Tushratta. His son, Shattiwaza, was forced to flee into exile in the Hittite kingdom while a usurper, Shuttarna III, took the Mitanni throne. Shattiwaza married the daughter of the Hittite king and returned to retake Mitanni with the assistance of a Hittite army. As a result, the former Mitanni Empire became little more than a Hittite vassal state, and when it was attacked by the Assyrians, it quickly fell. This angered the Hittite king, and the Assyrians found themselves fighting the powerful Hittites. Neither side was able to gain a decisive advantage, and the two resumed an uneasy peace after several indecisive battles with the remnant of the Mitanni Empire remaining under Hittite control.

When Ashur-uballit I died in 1330 BCE, he left an Assyrian Empire that was larger and more powerful than anything that had gone before, and his descendants were to enlarge it even further. Ashur-uballit I was succeeded by his son, Enlil-nirari. The new king was immediately attacked by the Babylonian Empire under the command of King Kurigalzu II who Ashur-uballit I had placed on the throne. Enlil-nirari defeated the Babylonians in the battle of Sugagu and appropriated a great deal of former Babylonian territory for Assyria.

When Enlil-nirari died in 1319 BCE, he was succeeded by his son Arik-den-ili who expanded the Assyrian Empire even further, conquering parts of the Zagros Mountains after battles with the Gutians and the Lullibi. He also conquered parts of Syria, defeating the Semitic Ahlamu people. The Assyrian kings who followed conquered more lands, mainly those that had been occupied by the Hittites and the Hurrians but also pushing back the frontier of the Babylonian Empire even further to the south.

In 1274 BCE, a new Assyrian king was crowned—Shalmaneser I. He proved just as hungry for conquest as his predecessors, completely destroying what remained of the Mitanni Empire and defeating the Hittite and the Aramaean allies of the Mitanni in the process. He also successfully led campaigns against the Hurrian kingdom of Urartu in Eastern Anatolia and the Caucasus Mountains, and he defeated the Gutians in the Zagros Mountains. The Hittites, fearful of the growing power of the Assyrians, formed an alliance with the Babylonians to try to limit its growth by imposing economic sanctions. This was a failure—Assyria still controlled most of the important trade routes, and wealth continued to flow into the empire. Shalmaneser I undertook many significant building projects during his reign, including substantial expansion and improvements in the new city of Kalhu.

The next king of Assyria, Tukulti-Ninurta I, came to the throne in 1244 BCE and reigned for more than 30 years. He completely conquered Babylon and installed himself as king of Babylon (his other titles included king of Karduniash, king of Sumer and Akkad, king of Sippar, and king of Tilmun and Meluhha). Many scholars believe that

Tukulti-Ninurta I was the historic origin of the character Nimrod in the Old Testament of the Bible. Tukulti-Ninurta I oversaw the building of yet another new capital for the Assyrian Empire, Kar-Tukulti-Ninurta, just to the north of Ashur, and this became the location for a new temple complex dedicated to the god Ashur.

Tukulti-Ninurta was murdered by his sons circa 1207 BCE and one of them, Ashur-nadin-apli, became the new king. Ashur-nadin-apli was more interested in enjoying the luxuries of his new lifestyle than expanding the empire, and he left the day-to-day running of provinces to governors. Babylon took advantage of the king's inattention to make a successful bid for independence. Following the death of Ashur-nadin-apli after just a few years as king, there was a period of internal turmoil in Assyria, and the three subsequent kings ruled for a period of just 14 years in total.

Happily for the Assyrians, the next king, Ashur-dan I, remained in power for more than 40 years and brought back stability to the region. Under his rule, Assyria re-occupied northern Babylon and waged a successful war against the kingdom of Elam. After Ashur-dan's death in 1134 BCE, a series of kings ruled before the ascension of Tiglath-Pileser I in 1115 BCE. This king ruled for about 38 years, and his reign would see the Assyrian Empire achieve its greatest extent and power to this point in time.

The new king's first campaign was against the Phrygians, a people who had migrated from the Balkans to an area of southwest Anatolia. These people had started to expand into areas of Upper Mesopotamia that had formerly been under the control of Assyria. They were quickly defeated by Tiglath-Pileser I who then expanded Assyrian territory even further by occupying lands formerly held by the Luwians in western Asia Minor. For the first five years of his rule, the new king kept his armies in almost constant action, taking lands from the Neo-Hittite Empire, from the Aramaeans in northern and central Syria, conquering a number of Canaanite-Phoenician cities to give access to the Mediterranean Sea, and quelling at least two rebellions by Babylon.

By the time that Tiglath-Pileser I died in 1076 BCE, the Assyrian Empire was the most powerful in the region. His son, Asharid-apal-Ekur, ruled for just two years before being succeeded by Ashur-bel-kala, whose reign would mark the beginning of the final decline for the Middle Assyrian Empire. Around 1060 BCE, Assyria was rocked by a ferocious civil war when Tukulti-Mer, a usurper who wanted to claim the throne, gathered an army and attacked the king. Ashur-bel-kala was able to defeat this threat, but the fighting meant that the Assyrians were distracted from maintaining control over the lands they had conquered. Before Ashur-bel-kala's death in 1056 BCE, Assyria had lost many of the lands conquered from the Canaanites and Phoenicians as well as Aramaean territory in Syria.

The core cities of the empire were still safe, and Assyria controlled a large proportion of all trade in the area, but the empire was considerably smaller than it had previously been.

Chapter Five

The Warrior Society

"Tell me your friends, and I'll tell you who you are."

—Mesopotamian proverb

Before moving on to examine the next phase of the history of the Assyrian Empire, it is worth pausing for a moment to consider the importance of the army in this history. In the previous chapters, you have read how Assyrian forces conquered almost every enemy they encountered—in fact, there are very few accounts of the defeat of Assyrian forces in the empire's early history. Why was this? What was it about Assyrian military forces that made them so successful and so feared?

There are several strands to this answer. One is equipment—Assyrian artisans and metalworkers were amongst the best and most advanced in the ancient world. The iron weapons and armor provided to Assyrian forces were simply better than those used by their adversaries. They were also cheaper and easier to produce. In many battles, the Assyrians faced opponents in whose armies only the aristocratic leaders had sophisticated weapons and armor. In the Assyrian army, every infantry and cavalry soldier was equipped with iron weapons and armor. Assyrian armies were also the first to incorporate a corps of engineers who were adept at producing rams, scaling ladders, towers, and other equipment that could be used to assault the walled cities of their enemies. These factors would give any military force an advantage, but they don't completely explain the string of virtually uninterrupted Assyrian victories.

Another factor was conscription. Every male Assyrian citizen, regardless of rank or religion, was required to serve for a fixed period in the army. This meant that, in time of war, large numbers of trained reservists could be called up to bolster the size of the army. The fact that its soldiers were trained also gave the Assyrians a distinct advantage on the battlefield. Most ancient armies would simply fling themselves en masse at the enemy; the Assyrians were able to use formations and tactics considerably more sophisticated than this.

The army was a powerful factor in Assyrian society. Warriors were respected. Kings were expected to lead their armies and to display physical strength and courage, and many state offices were controlled by the military. However, having a largely conscript army also had its disadvantages. Most of the men serving in the army were farmers. Calling up large numbers of farmers during the planting or harvesting season would have caused food shortages, so early Assyrian campaigns were generally conducted only in the summer, after the crops had been planted and before they were due to be harvested. There were essentially no wars during the winter.

King Tiglath-Pileser III was one of the first Assyrian leaders to recognize that having a fulltime, professional army capable of campaigning all year round would give a distinct military advantage. Under his reign during the Neo-

Assyrian Empire, the Assyrian army was completely reorganized as a professional force which gave it an even greater advantage on the battlefield.

There was another weapon that the Assyrians used with great success: fear. All Assyrian leaders and military forces displayed extreme cruelty and brutality, particularly to those they had defeated. In cities that had stood against the Assyrians, captives were frequently executed in public in the most barbaric ways. For example, one of the kings of the Neo-Assyrian Empire noted that, following the re-conquest of the rebellious city of Suru on the Euphrates River, "I built a pillar at the city gate and I flayed all the chief men who had revolted and I covered the pillar with their skins; some I walled up inside the pillar, some I impaled upon the pillar on stakes."

Many Assyrian commemorative engravings show the most horrific treatment of captives. Being skinned alive was not uncommon, nor was impalement, castration, and having one's tongue torn out. Captured women and children were sometimes burned alive, and the heads of executed captives were often displayed on or near the walls of captured cities as a warning to others. When approaching a city that was about to be besieged, the Assyrians would often offer the opportunity to surrender. If this was accepted, the city and its inhabitants would be spared. If it was not, those inside could expect no mercy if they failed to defend themselves against the Assyrians. In these circumstances, the Assyrian army's reputation for cruelty and brutality served it well, and many cities surrendered without a fight rather than face the consequences of resistance.

The Assyrians also used routinely used mass deportation as an instrument of repression. A captured city might be completely destroyed and all its survivors marched off into another region. Those who had stood against the Assyrians were sold into slavery, and the remainder were shipped off to other areas where they might eventually be absorbed into Assyrian society.

While their reputation for cruelty may have helped in military conquest, it also caused problems for the Assyrians. Mass executions, dismemberment, and the mutilation and deportation of captives left a legacy of hatred and distrust throughout conquered territories. Little wonder that rebellions were almost constant in parts of the Assyrian Empire.

Chapter Six

The Late Bronze Age Collapse

"Within a period of forty to fifty years at the end of the thirteenth and the beginning of the twelfth century almost every significant city in the eastern Mediterranean world was destroyed, many of them never to be occupied again."

—Robert Drews

From approximately 1200 to 900 BCE, there was a time of social disintegration and change which has become known to historians as the Late Bronze Age Collapse. In a period of just 50 years, the Hittite Empire collapsed, as did the Kassite Dynasty in Babylon, the Egyptian Empire, and the Amorite Empire, and there was chaos in the lands controlled by Canaan. Almost every city-state between the Greek city of Pylos and the Palestinian city of Gaza was destroyed and abandoned during this period. Many were never rebuilt.

A new people appeared in this time—the Sea Peoples, a confederation of seafaring people who ravaged the crumbling Egyptian Empire and many other lands east of the Mediterranean Sea. Historians argue about where these people came from (or if they even existed as a coherent federation), but there is no doubt that many civilizations in this period were destroyed or at least destabilized by marauders from the sea.

There have been many theories suggested explaining this sudden, catastrophic collapse. One involves long-term climate change caused by a fall in surface sea levels in the North Atlantic, leading to reduced rainfall and drought throughout the Middle East. The eruption of the volcano Hekla 3 in Iceland has also been suggested as a possible contributory factor. This massive eruption threw so much volcanic debris into the atmosphere that it may have caused a global cooling that could have lasted for up to 20 years. Another suggestion is that this decline was caused by a "general systems collapse" where the increasing complexity, sophistication, and inter-dependence of emerging technologies proved too fragile to sustain and led to an involuntary return to a simpler way of life.

Whatever its cause, the collapse was sudden and widespread, and it has been described as the worst disaster in ancient history. Many cities were abandoned, literacy levels dropped dramatically, trade routes that had operated for hundreds of years ceased, and famine, drought, and population movement were widespread.

Assyria was affected by this collapse, but not as dramatically as many other empires in the region. After the death of King Ashur-bel-kala in 1056 BCE, the Assyrian Empire entered a period of slow decline for more than 100 years. Semitic-speaking people including the Chaldeans, Arameans, and Suteans occupied lands to the south and west which had formerly been controlled by Assyria, including Babylon. People from Iran, including the Persians, Medes, Sarmatians, and Parthians, moved into lands in the east. In the north, the resurgent Phrygians overran former Hittite lands. The Assyrians escaped the attentions of the Sea Peoples, mainly because their reduced empire had no major seaports and no access to the Mediterranean Sea.

By 1000 BCE, the Assyrian Empire comprised only lands close to the core cities, but importantly, the Assyrians still controlled all the main trade routes with central Mesopotamia, northwestern Iran, eastern Aramea, and southeastern Asia Minor. Control of these vital routes allowed the empire to retain coherence at a time when many other potential competitors were disintegrating.

The Assyrian kings who ruled during the one hundred years following the death of Ashur-bel-kala maintained a generally sensible policy of defending the borders of the core Assyrian homelands and the territories immediately surrounding these while mounting only the occasional limited, punitive raid against any incursion into their territory. These kings included Eriba-Adad II, Ashurnasirpal I, Ashur-rabi II, and Tiglath-Pileser II. They are not remembered in the same way as Assyrian kings who led successful campaigns of conquest, but this comparison is unfair; their policy of simply maintaining the empire at a time when so much around them was disintegrating was an essential step towards ensuring that, when the effects of the Bronze Age Collapse began to lessen, the Assyrians would be in a good position to resume their domination of the region.

Chapter Seven

The Neo-Assyrian Empire

"We, the Assyrians, have contributed to the world the greatest of all times: wisdom. We ought to be proud and continue sharing our talents with mankind."

—Misha Ashoorian

The beginning of the Neo-Assyrian Empire is generally agreed to have been marked by the ascension to the throne of King Adad-nirari II in 911 BCE. His father, Ashur-dan II, had been content to focus on restoring Assyria to its natural borders, but the new king was intent on expansion from the very beginning.

His first targets were lands occupied by Aramean and Hurrian people to the north of Assyria. These were quickly conquered, and large numbers of prisoners were deported to provide a workforce for Assyrian trade and agriculture. Next, Adad-nirari II turned his attention back to the south, to the ever-troublesome Babylonian Empire. He formed an alliance with the city-states of Hindanu and Laqe to the northwest of Babylon and attacked the forces of the Babylonian king, Shamash-mudammiq. The Assyrians and their allies were successful, and a large area of land north of the Diyala River which included the towns of Hit and Zanqu was occupied. Rather than trying to completely crush Babylon, an alliance was formed between the two empires, which was cemented by each king agreeing for his daughter to be married to the other. Although the alliance was nominally an equal one, the growing military power of Assyria meant that, in reality, the Babylonian Empire became weaker and a less significant force in Mesopotamia.

Adad-nirari II also spent time strengthening Assyrian rule over adjacent lands. Control had loosened during the preceding 100 years, and the new king reversed this trend to ensure that, by the time that he died in 891 BCE, Assyria was firmly in control of a large swath of territory. Adad-nirari II was succeeded by his son, Tukulti-Ninurta II, who continued his father's program of conquest, mounting successful campaigns against the Aramean king of Bit-Zamani and against the tribes of the Zagros Mountains. Tukulti-Ninurta II also expanded and improved the cities of Ashur and Nineveh, building new temples and improving both cities' defenses. Tukulti-Ninurta II died in 884 BCE after just seven years as king, and it was left to his son and successor, Ashurnasirpal II to undertake the most ambitious plans for the expansion of the empire.

Expansion to the north quickly pushed the limits of Assyrian control as far as the city of Nairi in the Aramean Highlands. Then the new king attacked, subjugated, and extracted tribute from the kingdom of Phrygia in Anatolia and crushed the kingdom of Aram in modern-day Syria. Remaining Hittite tribes between the Euphrates and Khabur Rivers were wiped out, and Assyrian troops reached as far as the Mediterranean kingdom of Phoenicia which they conquered and from which they were able to extract tribute.

Ashurnasirpal II quickly developed a reputation for extreme brutality, especially towards those who attempted to rebel against Assyrian rule. An inscription has been discovered which describes the king's brutal and violent reaction to one such revolt: "Their men young and old I took prisoners. Of some I cut off their feet and hands; of others I cut off the ears noses and lips; of the young men's ears I made a heap; of the old men's heads I made a minaret. I exposed their heads as a trophy in front of their city. The male children and the female children I burned in flames; the city I destroyed, and consumed with fire."

When he returned to Assyria, Ashurnasirpal II relocated the capital to the city of Kalhu where he used prisoners taken during his military campaigns to build new temples and palaces. The royal palace at Kalhu was completed in 879 BCE and became the administrative and political center of the Assyrian Empire.

Ashurnasirpal II died in 859 BCE and was succeeded by his son, Shalmaneser III, who ruled for 35 years and continued the conquests started by his father. During his reign, Babylon was finally occupied, the city of Damascus was besieged and forced to pay tribute, Jehu, the king of Israel was forced to accept Assyrian domination, and the Phoenician states of Sidon and Tyre were brought under direct Assyrian control. By the time that Shalmaneser III completed his military campaigns, Assyria was the most powerful empire in the known world, exerting control over the Near East, the eastern Mediterranean, most of Asia Minor, the Caucasus Mountains, and even parts of the Arabian Peninsula and North Africa.

The final years of Shalmaneser's rule were marred by the rebellion of his son Ashur-nadin-aplu and a subsequent civil war that came close to tearing Assyria apart. While the Assyrians fought amongst themselves, many of the lands they had brought under control took the opportunity to rebel. The Babylonians in the south were the first to shake off Assyrian control, and this encouraged the Medes and Persians in the north and east and the Arameans and Neo-Hittites in the west to also rise against the Assyrians. When Shalmaneser III died in 824 BCE, the civil war was continuing, and it was left to his second son and successor, Shamshi-Adad V, not just to crush the rebellion but to reconquer the lands who had tried to break free of Assyrian control.

When Shamshi-Adad V died unexpectedly in 811 BCE, his young son Adad-nirari II became king. The boy was so young that it seems that his mother, Shammuramat, may have ruled on his behalf until he took control in 806 BCE. Adad-nirari II did his best to restore the empire to its former size and power, mounting campaigns in the Levant, Damascus, and in Iran as far as the Caspian Sea.

The premature death of Adad-nirari II in 783 BCE led to a series of relatively ineffective rulers (Shalmaneser IV, Ashur-dan III, and Ashur-nirari V) and 40 years of internal revolt and the rebellion of occupied territories. This was exacerbated by a plague that swept the country, and by 745 BCE, the Assyrian Empire was in serious trouble. Disease and civil war had reduced the once-mighty empire to ruins, and even the capital, Kalhu, had joined with the rebels. Then an Assyrian general named Pulu staged a coup, seized the throne, and named himself King Tiglath-Pileser III.

Tiglath-Pileser III first crushed the rebellion and then immediately made sweeping and significant changes. The army was changed from being a seasonal, conscript force to a standing professional army capable of campaigning at any time of year. Conquered territories were administered under a new bureaucracy which was responsible directly to the king for tribute and an annual contribution towards maintaining the army. With his new army, Tiglath-Pileser III set about reconquering those lands which had attempted to break free of Assyrian control during the period of civil war. Babylon was attacked and subdued, the Medes and Persians were defeated, and the Neo-Hittites were brought back under Assyrian control. Tiglath-Pileser III also led a successful invasion of the kingdom Israel and forced it to pay an annual tribute to Assyria.

Tiglath-Pileser III died in 727 BCE, and the throne passed to his son Shalmaneser V. The new king continued his father's military conquests, but died in unknown circumstances in 722 BCE while supervising a siege of the Israeli city of Samaria. The Assyrian throne was then claimed by Shalmaneser V's brother who named himself King Sargon II. The new king started a dynasty that would lead the Assyrian Empire to its greatest extent and power. Sargon II consolidated Assyria's hold over captured territories and expanded into the lands of Elam. He also occupied the city of Babylon and had himself crowned king of Babylon and built yet another capital city, Dur-Sharrukin ("Fortress of Sargon"), near the existing city of Nineveh.

Sargon II died in battle in 705 BCE and was succeeded by his son Sennacherib. Sennacherib installed his son and heir, Ashur-nadin-shumi, as king of Babylon, but when he was murdered by Elamite plotters and an Elamite king was placed on the Babylonian throne, this provoked a long-running war between Babylon and Assyria. Neither side was able to completely defeat the other and, after a devastating series of engagements which continued for four years, the two agreed to a peace agreement.

Still, the Assyrian king never forgot or forgave the murder of his son, and in 689 BCE, Sennacherib took advantage of a dispute over the succession in Elam to attack and completely destroy the city of Babylon. He also destroyed the temple to the god Marduk at the center of the city and brought the statue of the god from that temple back to Nineveh. This act of sacrilege horrified even the Assyrian people, who shared many gods with the Babylonians, and in 681 BCE, Sennacherib was murdered by his own eldest sons, reputedly as a punishment for his defiling the temple and stealing the statue of Marduk.

There followed a brief civil war in Assyria as the sons who had murdered Sennacherib fought with his youngest son, Esarhaddon, for the succession. Esarhaddon was victorious, and one of his first acts as the new king of Assyria was to rebuild the city of Babylon and the desecrated temple of Marduk. Esarhaddon then turned his attention to conquest and succeeded in mounting an invasion of Egypt that removed the Nubian-Kushite rule in Egypt and completely destroyed the powerful Kushite Empire. In 669 BCE, Esarhaddon suddenly became ill and died, leaving his two sons to vie for the throne of Assyria.

His formal heir was his younger son Ashurbanipal, who was declared king upon his father's death. However, his eldest son, Shamash-shum-ukin, who had been made king of Babylon, was not willing to accept the authority of his younger brother. Although Ashurbanipal campaigned successfully against the Medes in the east and fought against several rebellions in Egypt, he was never entirely free of the fear that his brother would attempt to raise Babylon against Assyria. In 652 BCE, Shamash-shum-ukin raised a huge rebellion against his brother, led by Babylon and aimed at toppling Ashurbanipal from the throne of Assyria. The revolt included the Elamites, the Arabs, and the Chaldeans who all united with Babylon against Assyria. The vassal pharaoh of Egypt seized this opportunity to announce Egyptian independence from Assyria, though he was careful not to take sides in the civil war.

The war between Ashurbanipal and Shamash-shum-ukin raged for four years, leaving large areas of Mesopotamia devastated and depopulated. It finally ended in 648 BCE when Assyrian troops took Babylon and Shamash-shum-ukin set fire to the royal palace, killing himself in the process. Ashurbanipal then turned on those who had supported his brother. He invaded the Arabian Peninsula and killed the Arab kings Abiate and Uate. The Chaldean tribes in the southeast of Mesopotamia were attacked, defeated, and placed under Assyrian control. Elam was attacked and its capital, Susa, was sacked.

By 640 BCE, Ashurbanipal was the leader of the largest empire in the world. Every other potential internal or external rival had been either destroyed or was forced to pay tribute to the might of the Assyrian Empire. On paper at least, the empire looked stronger, more powerful, and larger than it had ever been. The truth, however, was rather different.

Chapter Eight

The Fall of the Assyrian Empire

"I need not fear my enemies because the most they can do is attack me. I need not fear my friends because the most they can do is betray me. But I have much to fear from people who are indifferent."

—Mesopotamian proverb

Although the Assyrian Empire which Ashurbanipal ruled was bigger than it had ever been, it was also in a much more precarious position. The internal strife and civil wars combined with almost constant campaigning to expand the borders of the empire had left Assyria short of manpower for its armies and short of the resources required to keep a large standing army equipped and fed. Many of the provinces from which tribute could be expected had been devastated during the civil wars and were unable to contribute significantly to the maintenance of the empire. Even the sheer size and geographic spread of the empire made it difficult for the king to maintain direct control. Many vassal states and even supposed allies began to wonder whether it might be possible to make a bid for independence. Somehow King Ashurbanipal was able to hold the tottering empire together during his lifetime, but when he died circa 627 BCE, the empire disintegrated more quickly than anyone could have foreseen.

The initial problem was, once again, internal strife. Ashurbanipal was succeeded by his son, Ashur-etil-ilani. The new king reigned for about three years—the absence of records from this period make it very difficult to be precise. It seems that he was deposed as a result of a coup staged by one of the Assyrian generals, Sin-shumu-lishir, who first had himself crowned king of Babylon and then launched an attack on Assyria which led to him taking the crown. He was opposed in a continuing civil war by Sin-shar-ishkun. Fighting between factions was bitter and protracted, but around 626 BCE, Sin-shar-ishkun was able to take the throne. He would be the last Assyrian king to rule over an empire.

While Assyria was being weakened further by another civil war, many of the states which had previously been under its control took the opportunity to become independent. In 625 BCE, a Chaldean, Nabopolassar, became king of Babylon following an uprising there. He declared Babylon to be independent of Assyria, and Sin-shar-ishkun was forced to raise an army and march on Babylon. Before he had a chance to defeat the rebellious Babylonians, another insurrection broke out, and a usurper tried to take the Assyrian throne. Sin-shar-ishkun was forced to send part of his army back to the Assyrian homelands to quell this revolt, but these troops instead changed sides and joined the insurrection. The king was forced to return with his whole army to put down this threat to his rule, leaving the Babylonians to become even stronger.

By 620 BCE, Nabopolassar had consolidated his rule over the Babylonian Empire and completely driven the Assyrians out. At the same time, the Medes in the northwest rebelled against Assyrian rule and created a new, independent kingdom which in time would become the Persian Empire. The Scythians were a nomadic and warlike people from the western Eurasian Steppe who had previously been under Assyrian control. They too seized this opportunity to retake control of their own lands and to make incursions in areas that had previously been Assyrian vassal states. The Cimmerians were a people of Iranian origin who had previously come under Assyrian domination in Anatolia. They used the weakness of the Assyrian Empire as an opportunity to rebel.

In 616 BCE, Nabopolassar, king of Babylon, made an alliance with the Median king, Cyaxares, against Assyria, and the Scythians and Cimmerians were persuaded to join. Suddenly, Assyria was facing overwhelming numbers of enemies on every side. For four years, bitter fighting between the forces of this confederation and the Assyrians led to a gradual reduction in Assyrian territory until, in 612 BCE, the city of Nineveh was taken and sacked and King Sin-shar-ishkun was killed.

A new Assyrian king, Ashur-uballit II, was crowned, but he inherited little but the tattered remains of the once-mighty empire. He was a general in the Assyrian army, though some historians believe that he may also have been the brother of Sin-shar-ishkun. Ashur-uballit II managed to fight his way out of Nineveh while it was besieged and moved to the city of Harran, an ancient city and a trading center of Upper Mesopotamia. He declared this the new capital of the Assyrian Empire, but his reign there was short.

He was able to make an alliance with Egypt, which provided him with troops and much-needed supplies and resources but, in 609 BCE, a force of Babylonians, Medes, and Scythians attacked and sacked Harran. It is not known whether Ashur-uballit II was killed at this time or whether he managed to escape from the besieged city, but the fall of this city marked the end of the Assyrian Empire and the effective end of Assyria as an independent state.

Conclusion

At the height of its power, the Assyrian Empire covered an astounding area. It completely incorporated lands that make up the modern countries of Egypt, Syria, Iraq, Israel, Lebanon, Palestine, Kuwait, Jordan, Bahrain, and Cyprus. It also covered large parts of modern Iran, Sudan, Saudi Arabia, Libya, Turkey, and Armenia. At the time, it was the largest and most powerful empire the world had seen, and following the emergence of the Neo-Assyrian Empire after the Bronze Age Collapse, it had few serious rivals in the area.

Yet the very size and extent of the empire contained the seeds of its own destruction. It proved to be impossible to effectively govern and suppress potential rebellions over such a large area. Creating a large, professional, standing army certainly gave the Assyrians a distinct advantage on the battlefield, but the costs of maintaining an army large enough to control the territory of the empire proved to be beyond the capacity of the Assyrians, and the empire was riven by continuing revolts and insurrections which were costly to suppress.

The end of the Assyrian Empire, like the destruction of so many empires before and after, came not from enemies from the outside, but because of internal problems. The latter period of the Assyrian Empire was marked by a series of civil wars, which distracted leaders from the business of governing the empire and used resources that might otherwise have been used to maintain control over vassal states.

While it was ruled by men of strong will who were willing to use extreme brutality to deter those who might have stood against them, it was possible to hold the empire together. When the throne passed to men of lesser will and perhaps lesser abilities, the Assyrian Empire simply disintegrated under the weight of its own success.

68563721R00027